COLIN POWELL

A Real-Life Reader Biography

Stacey Granger

Mitchell Lane Publishers, Inc.
P.O. Box 619
Bear, Delaware 19701
http://www.mitchelllane.com

Printing   1   2   3   4   5   6   7   8   9

Real-Life Reader Biographies

Paula Abdul	Christina Aguilera	Marc Anthony	Lance Armstrong
Drew Barrymore	Tony Blair	Brandy	Garth Brooks
Kobe Bryant	Sandra Bullock	Mariah Carey	Aaron Carter
Cesar Chavez	Roberto Clemente	Christopher Paul Curtis	Roald Dahl
Oscar De La Hoya	Trent Dimas	Celine Dion	Sheila E.
Gloria Estefan	Mary Joe Fernandez	Michael J. Fox	Andres Galarraga
Sarah Michelle Gellar	Jeff Gordon	Virginia Hamilton	Mia Hamm
Melissa Joan Hart	Salma Hayek	Jennifer Love Hewitt	Faith Hill
Hollywood Hogan	Katie Holmes	Enrique Iglesias	Allen Iverson
Janet Jackson	Derek Jeter	Steve Jobs	Alicia Keys
Michelle Kwan	Bruce Lee	Jennifer Lopez	Cheech Marin
Ricky Martin	Mark McGwire	Alyssa Milano	Mandy Moore
Chuck Norris	Tommy Nuñez	Rosie O'Donnell	Mary-Kate and Ashley Olsen
Rafael Palmeiro	Gary Paulsen	**Colin Powell**	Freddie Prinze, Jr.
Condoleezza Rice	Julia Roberts	Robert Rodriguez	J.K. Rowling
Keri Russell	Winona Ryder	Cristina Saralegui	Charles Schulz
Arnold Schwarzenegger	Selena	Maurice Sendak	Dr. Seuss
Shakira	Alicia Silverstone	Jessica Simpson	Sinbad
Jimmy Smits	Sammy Sosa	Britney Spears	Julia Stiles
Ben Stiller	Sheryl Swoopes	Shania Twain	Liv Tyler
Robin Williams	Vanessa Williams	Venus Williams	Tiger Woods

Library of Congress Cataloging-in-Publication Data
Granger, Stacey, 1969-
        Colin Powell / Stacey Granger.
                p. cm. — (A real-life reader biography)
        Includes index.
        Summary: A biography of Colin Powell, who overcame poverty and prejudice to become a four-star general, Chairman of the Joint Chiefs of Staff, and Secretary of State.
        ISBN 1-58415-144-7
        1. Powell, Colin L.—Juvenile literature. 2. Generals—United States—Biography—Juvenile literature. 3. African American generals—Biography—Juvenile literature. 4. United States Army—Biography—Juvenile literature. [1. Powell, Colin L. 2. Cabinet officers. 3. Generals. 4. African Americans—Biography.] I. Title. II. Series.
E849.5P68 G73 2003
327.73'0092—dc21
        [B]
                                                                                                200202

ABOUT THE AUTHOR: Born and raised in Michigan, Stacey Granger now lives in a small town in Maryland near the Chesapeake Bay. A frequent contributor to anthology collections such as *Chicken Soup for the Soul*, she is also the author of three books and does freelance writing for her local paper.

PHOTO CREDITS: Cover: Walter Weissman/Globe Photos, Inc.; p. 4 Mark Wilson/Getty Images; p. 6 AFP/Corbis; p. Manny Ceneta/Getty Images; p. 17 Wally McNamee/Corbis; p. 20 AP Photo/MTI/Attila Kovacs; p. 27 AP Photo/U.S. Department of Defense/Robert D. Ward; p. 30 John Barrett/Globe Photos

ACKNOWLEDGMENTS: The following story has been thoroughly researched, and to the best of our knowledge, represents a true story. While every possible effort has been made to ensure accuracy, the publisher will not assume liability for damages caused by inaccuracies in the data, and makes no warranty on the accuracy of the information contained herein. This story has not been authorized nor endorsed by Colin Powell.

Table of Contents

Chapter 1
The Young Drifter

Colin Powell's life was going nowhere. For a young African-American in the South Bronx area of New York City, that's not surprising. Even today, there is very little opportunity there. Back in the 1950s, when Powell was a teenager, the situation was even worse. Coupled with the mediocre grades he had achieved in high school, his chances for success dropped even further.

Powell confesses that at that point in his life he was directionless. "My pleasures were hanging out with the guys, and 'making the walk' down nearby streets," he says in his best-selling autobiography, *My American Journey*.

But even those very modest ambitions weren't entirely successful.

Being from South Bronx in the 1950s meant Colin Powell's chances for success were low.

In the late 1990s, many Americans wanted Colin Powell to run for President of the United States.

"Usually, the other guys looked on me, not quite as a sissy, but as a 'nice' kid, even a bit of a mama's boy," he recalls.

He had also played basketball, run on the track team, tried to play musical instruments and joined the Boy Scouts for a while. But none of those activities gave him much satisfaction or a feeling of belonging. He couldn't seem to stick with anything long enough to become good at it.

So it wasn't surprising that the future looked very bleak to young Colin Powell.

Unlike many of his peers, at least he had graduated from high school. But he had only managed a low C average and was barely accepted into City College of New York (CCNY). Even after his first semester, doubts about his ability to do his schoolwork had him nearly convinced to drop out.

If that had happened, he might have become just another face in the crowd, another young African-American facing a dismal future.

But he didn't drop out. And soon he would discover a purpose and direction for his life. Eventually he would become renowned throughout the world. Many of his countrymen even wanted him to run for this nation's highest office, the President of the United States.

"You've done well," a Congresswoman in Washington, DC said to him after he had delivered a statement to the subcommittee of which she was a member.

And Powell, the son of two immigrants who came to this country almost penniless, replied, "I ain't done bad."

If Colin had dropped out of college, he might have become just another face in the crowd.

Chapter 2
A South Bronx Boyhood

Colin's parents both grew up in Jamaica, though they never met there.

Colin Powell's story begins in Jamaica, an island about the size of Connecticut located about 500 miles south of Florida in the Caribbean Sea. That was where his parents grew up, though they never met while they were living there.

Colin Powell's mother, Maud Ariel McKoy, or Arie as she was known, was the eldest of nine children. Her parents eventually separated, and her mother found work in Panama, then Cuba, and finally settled in the bustling city of New York, where opportunities were better. Arie soon joined her.

While Arie graduated from high school before going to work, Luther Theophilus Powell, Colin's father, never finished his education. As he reached manhood in the 1920's there was very little opportunity for a promising future in Jamaica. The colorful tales of life in America attracted Luther, and he left his family and home behind to seek a better life. He traveled first to Connecticut, finding work as a gardener before moving south to Harlem, New York. Many Jamaicans, Cubans, and other West Indians already lived there.

Two of those Jamaicans were Arie McKoy and her mother, who took in boarders in addition to raising her own children. One of the boarders was Luther Powell. Not long after they met, Luther proposed and they were married soon afterward.

When Colin was four, America entered World War II.

After their marriage, Arie and Luther made a home in a pleasant neighborhood in Harlem and commuted to the garment district in central Manhattan. Arie worked as a seamstress and Luther was a shipping clerk. Eventually he would become head of the shipping department.

Marilyn Powell was their first child, born in 1931. Colin Luther Powell would join the family on April 5, 1937, born at the Presbyterian Hospital in Harlem.

When Colin was four, America entered World War II. He and his friends would "play war" in the streets, showering each other with

imaginary bullets and scanning the skies for fighter planes over American soil.

By then, Luther had made the decision to

Colin at a hearing on foreign policy budget

move his family out of Harlem, where crime had begun to rise. In 1943, when Colin was six years old, the Powell family moved into an apartment at 952 Kelly Street, in the Hunts Point section of the South Bronx. Although Luther had wanted to raise his family in a better area, even on Kelly Street crime was on the rise. The families living in the Bronx were forced to brace their doors against burglaries, and watched as street fights and knifings occurred. Even so, Colin was very happy in the Bronx, and thought of Kelly Street, which was home to many of his relatives, as his whole world.

By the time Colin turned nine, while attending school at P.S. 39, he had been labeled a "Four Up," which branded him as a slow learner. This devastated Colin's family, as Marilyn, Colin's sister, had already been marked an excellent student, with college definitely in her future. Education was the surest way to a better life for children in the West Indian community. To be termed a slow learner was somewhat disappointing. Today Colin Powell describes himself in those days by saying, "I lacked drive, not ability. Though I was amenable, I was also aimless."

It was typical of his life to that point. His sister had gone to one of New York's finest high schools, but when Colin sought admission to another good school, his guidance counselor wrote back with a simple note: "We advise against it." He wound up attending nearby Morris High School, which basically accepted anyone.

Things might have looked more promising for young Colin if he had had some degree of athletic ability. Yet he describes himself as "not much of an athlete." He wanted to make his father proud, and it was always painful to Colin that he seemed to disappoint Luther. Today, Colin says, "I imagined a pressure that was probably not

> **By the time he was nine, Colin was labeled a "Four Up," which branded him as a slow learner.**

there, since he (Luther) rarely uttered a word of reproach to me."

At the age of 16, just shy of his 17th birthday, Colin graduated from Morris with what he calls "poor grades." An average C student, he was unsure of his future. But he enrolled at City College of New York (CCNY) as an engineering major, which his mother encouraged him to do for the money.

He did surprisingly well in his first semester. This was mainly because he had yet to enroll in any engineering courses. But after taking an especially difficult class in mechanical drawing, Colin discovered he was not cut out to be an engineer.

"One hot afternoon," Colin says, "the instructor asked us to draw a cone intersecting a plane in space. The other students all began to draw, while I sat there staring into space. I could not, for the life of me, visualize a cone intersecting a plane in space. If this was engineering, the game was over."

But for Colin Powell, a much more important "game" was about to begin.

Chapter 3
The Pershing Rifles

He began his second year at CCNY with two changes. One was his decision to switch from engineering to geology, a choice that was unpopular with his parents. They could not understand why he would choose a major with so little future promise.

"There goes Colin again," they said. "Can't stick with anything."

The other change, in terms of his future, was far more important.

It had begun during the previous fall semester when the young men who were members of the Reserve Officers' Training Corps, or ROTC, caught Colin's attention. They dressed in smart uniforms, which struck a responsive chord. He was especially impressed by one of them.

The previous fall the young men who were members of the ROTC caught Colin's attention.

"Ronald Brooks was a young black man, tall, trim, handsome, the son of a Harlem Baptist preacher and possessed of a maturity beyond most college students," Powell says. "Ronnie was only two years older than I, but something in him commanded deference. And unlike me, Ronnie, a chemistry major, was a brilliant student. He was a cadet leader in the ROTC and an officer in the Pershing Rifles. He could drill men so that they moved like parts of a watch. Ronnie was sharp, quick, disciplined, organized, qualities then invisible in Colin Powell. I had found a model and a mentor. I set out to remake myself in the Ronnie Brooks mold."

So that fall, after stumbling through his first year of college, Colin Powell joined the ROTC.

The day he was issued the olive-drab suit, brown shirt and tie, brown pants and oversized cap he went home and dressed in his cadet uniform. Looking in the mirror, Colin remembers, "I liked what I saw."

But he didn't want to be just an average cadet. So he pledged himself to Ronald Brooks' group, the Pershing Rifles. They were the top unit in ROTC, and Powell felt a more serious commitment to a military career.

Colin Powell was no longer a young man without direction. He had found an organization that gave him a sense of belonging and a goal in life.

Journalist Juan Williams writes that the Army ROTC "was his gang, his team, his fraternity, his new extended family."

"For the first time in my life, I was a member of a brotherhood," Colin says. "Nothing I had been a part of, not the Boy Scouting, the basketball team or track team in high school had produced a sense of belonging. The PR's did that for me."

The deep commitment the PR's had toward one another, the selflessness, was what inspired Colin Powell to dedicate his future to being a soldier. He quickly became a leader.

Just as Ronnie Brooks was his role model, Powell became a role model for younger cadets. Eventually he was appointed commander of the Pershing Rifles and graduated at the top of the college's ROTC class of 1958 with the rank of cadet colonel, the highest rank in the corps.

Colin graduated at the top of the college's ROTC 1958 class with the rank of cadet colonel.

Chapter 4
The Young Soldier

Because Colin Powell left CCNY as a "Distinguished Military Graduate," the Army offered him a regular commission, rather than the customary reserve commission. It meant three years on active duty, not two. He eagerly accepted this honor.

In Georgia, Colin was banned from using the same restrooms as white people.

In June of 1958, 2nd Lieutenant Colin Powell arrived at Fort Benning, or "Old Rock" as it had been nicknamed during the Civil War. Fort Benning is over 182,000 acres of hilly landscape situated near Columbus, Georgia.

Colin had encountered little racial prejudice while growing up in the South Bronx or even within the confines of Fort Benning, but once outside the gates it was a different story. He was turned away from restaurants, and was banned from using the same restrooms as white people.

"Racism was still relatively new to me," Colin says. "I did not intend to give way to self-destructive rage, no matter how provoked. I did not feel inferior, and I was not going to let anybody make me believe I was. I occasionally felt hurt; I felt anger; but most of all I felt challenged. I'll show you!"

So Colin immersed himself in his training. He began with basic training, learning artillery fire, administrative procedures, avoiding capture, how to take prisoners, hand-to-hand combat, how to escape becoming a prisoner of

The Army gave Colin a sense of belonging.

war—basically how to survive as a soldier. Though he didn't realize it at the time, hauling 50-pound packs on his back through intense Georgian heat prepared Colin for the jungles in Vietnam, where he would soon serve.

He finished his basic training course in the top ten of his class and immediately followed this with Ranger school. He says, "If you were regular Army, you were infantry. If you were infantry, you wanted to be the best. The best meant being a Ranger and a paratrooper." Colin Powell was to become both.

During Ranger school he learned to jump from 250-foot towers, relying on a small parachute to save him from being smashed into a pulp. By his third week, he was jumping from airplanes, rappelling off cliffs, and sliding down a rope toward a tree at breakneck speed before being allowed to drop into the river below.

At the end of his training, Colin returned home for a visit. He was no longer just Colin Powell, but Colin Powell—Airborne Ranger, a title he was most proud of.

At the end of his training, Colin returned home as Colin Powell—Airborne Ranger.

Chapter 5
A Fateful Meeting

Fresh from Fort Benning, Colin was stationed in Germany for two years, then—by now a 1st lieutenant—reassigned to Fort Devens in Massachusetts, near Boston.

One November night in 1961 a buddy begged Colin to accompany him on a blind date. Begrudgingly, Colin accepted. His date turned out to be a soft-spoken young lady from Birmingham, Alabama named Alma Vivian Johnson. She attended Emerson College in Boston, where she was studying audiology as a graduate student.

Colin was smitten with Alma's friendly nature and beauty. Although she was attracted to Colin from the start, Alma was dismayed to discover he planned on making the Army his career. Even so, they continued

In November of 1961, a friend convinced Colin to accompany him on a blind date.

Colin with his wife Alma

to date. While their relationship bloomed, so did troubles in faraway Southeast Asia. The former French colony of Vietnam had been divided in half following the defeat of the French. The Communist North Vietnamese and rebellious Viet Cong in South Vietnam were trying to take over the entire country. So recently elected President John F. Kennedy began sending American military advisers to assist the South Vietnamese army.

By now, Colin had been promoted to captain, and

in August of 1962 he was delighted to find he was being sent to Vietnam that coming December. He immediately called Alma to share what he considered to be good news. He had been training for a real war, and this was his opportunity.

Her reaction shocked him.

"I'm not going to write to you," she told Colin. "We might as well end it now."

Alma was nearing 25 and had no intention of waiting around for Colin to return after a year. He spent a terrible night wondering about his intentions, and by morning he was on his way back to Boston to ask Alma to be his wife. She accepted and two weeks later, on August 25, 1962, they were married in Birmingham. Ronnie Brooks was Powell's best man. Colin met his bride's parents for the first time just 36 hours before the wedding.

Soon afterward, Colin was sent to Fort Bragg in North Carolina for a six-week training course to prepare him for Vietnam. Then he headed for Vietnam for a one-year tour of duty. Leaving Alma was especially difficult, as she was expecting their first child.

On August 25, 1962, Colin and Alma were married in Birmingham.

Chapter 6
Vietnam

Vietnam proved to be far worse than the summer Colin spent training in Georgia.

Vietnam proved to be far worse than the summer he spent training in Georgia. He fought clouds of insects, contended with leeches, was threatened by poisonous snakes and subjected to unpredictable weather. These unpleasantries didn't even include the punji spikes—bamboo stakes tipped with buffalo dung—or the ambushes that constantly lurked in the back of every soldier's mind. In July, Colin stepped on a punji spike. With his foot swollen to twice its normal size, he walked two hours back to camp. For this he was awarded the Purple Heart.

And all the while, Colin thought of Alma, especially during the spring when their child was due. Finally, word came through and Colin discovered he was a father. Michael

Kevin Powell was born March 23, 1963 in Birmingham.

Eight months later, Colin returned home, a war veteran, scarred in body and soul with the horrors of Vietnam, but eager to meet his son.

Michael was soon joined by Linda, who was born on April 16, 1965.

In 1967, Colin, now a major, was selected to attend the Army Command and General Staff College at Fort Leavenworth, Kansas. Working especially hard, he graduated second out of 1,244—a far cry from the "Four Up" who struggled to maintain a C average in high school.

Then he was sent to Vietnam for another year, where he was assigned to Major General Charles Gettys, who had personally requested that Powell become a member of his staff.

On November 16, 1968, a helicopter delivering Gettys, Powell and several other officers to their troops crashed on the mountainous terrain. Powell jumped from the wreckage with only a broken ankle, but he pulled Gettys, who was unconscious, from the wreck, then returned to help the others.

With a Legion of Merit medal and a firm sense of what had gone wrong for the U.S. in Vietnam, Colin returned to America in July of 1969.

Colin returned home from the war eager to meet his son.

Colin headed to George Washington University to get his masters degree in business administration.

"When we go to war, we should have a purpose that our people understand and support; we should mobilize the country's resources to fulfill that mission and then go in to win," he says.

Just over two decades later he would have his chance to put those words into effect.

But just then he had a more specific goal. He headed straight to George Washington University in Washington D.C. to get his masters degree in business administration.

By the time the Powells' third child, Annemarie, was born on May 20, 1971, Colin had been promoted to lieutenant colonel. Soon afterward, he was awarded his M.B.A. degree. From here it was off to the Pentagon to serve under General William H. Dupuy, the third most important Army officer there.

Chapter 7
A National Hero

One day, Colin received a call from the Infantry Branch Office, requesting he apply to be a White House Fellow. The position involved working in the White House for a year. He was among 1,500 who applied, and the oldest of the 17 who were selected. The position, which lasted from September 1972 through August 1973, provided invaluable lessons in the way that our government actually works. Powell would put this knowledge to good use in the future.

At the end of this term, soldiering called for Powell once more. In September 1973, he was sent to Korea, leaving Alma and his three children behind for another long year.

After returning to the States, Colin took a position at the Pentagon for a year until he

The Infantry Branch Office requested that Colin apply to be a White House Fellow.

Over the next ten years, Colin Powell learned the inner workings of political Washington.

was enrolled in the National War College, a prestigious appointment. By the time he graduated from the NWC, Colin was promoted to full colonel. He was appointed to Fort Campbell, in Kentucky, under General John Wickham, where he once again proved himself an extraordinary leader. But by July 1977, Washington would once again call Colonel Powell back into its fold.

For the next decade, Colin Powell learned the inner workings of political Washington.

But politics had nothing to do with a momentous event late in 1978. Powell was promoted to brigadier general.

"Promotion from lieutenant colonel to full colonel is a step up," Powell says. "From colonel to brigadier general is a giant leap. I did not take this promotion lightly. I acted more like a kid on Christmas morning."

Nearly a decade later, Colin, now a lieutenant general, was appointed National Security Advisor to President Ronald Reagan. This was a momentous achievement, as Colin Powell was the first African-American to ever hold this position. Two years later, Powell, now a four-star general, became the first African-American Chairman of the Joint Chiefs of Staff, this country's highest-ranking military officer.

But three days after the announcement, Powell heard some bad news. His old friend and mentor Ronnie Brooks, who had become a research chemist after fulfilling his military obligation, had died following a heart attack.

As he praised Brooks during the funeral, Colin wondered if his life would have turned out the way it did if the two men had never met.

In his role as JCS chairman, Colin guided and advised President George Bush and then President Bill Clinton through a number of international crises. His advice

Powell was the first African-American Chairman of the Joint Chiefs of Staff.

helped defeat Panamanian planning strongman Manuel Noriega during Operation Just Cause in December 1989.

But events the following summer brought him fully front and center into the national spotlight.

In August 1990 tens of thousands of troops from Iraq invaded neighboring Kuwait. Not only was it a case of unprovoked aggression, it also threatened vital U.S. interests in Saudi Arabia. Working closely with President Bush, Powell helped map America's retaliation. Through this planning, Powell was often referred to as "the Reluctant Warrior." Though many wanted America to charge into battle, Powell's duty as JCS Chairman was to present every alternative to war.

> **As JCS Chairman, Powell's duty was to present every alternative to war.**

Yet, in the end, firm commitment and excellent strategic planning under Powell's direction helped end the conflict in record time. Air strikes that lasted for slightly more than a month paved the way for a ground offensive that overwhelmed the Iraqis in just over four days. Very few Americans were killed or wounded. General "Stormin' Norman" Schwarzkopf, the U.S. field commander, became a national hero. So did Colin Powell.

Chapter 8
New Challenges

With so many life achievements and record-setting appointments, Colin Powell retired from the military after 35 years of service on September 30, 1993. He devoted his time to restoring old cars, writing his best-selling autobiography and speaking around the country and abroad.

As a civilian, Colin Powell began receiving awards, which eventually included two Presidential Medals of Freedom, the President's Citizens Medal, the Congressional Gold Medal, the Secretary of State Distinguished Service Medal, and the Secretary of Energy Distinguished Service Medal. Several schools and other institutions were named in his honor and universities and colleges across the country awarded him

After retiring, Powell devoted his time to restoring cars and writing his autobiography.

Colin at a book signing of his autobiography

honorary degrees. Queen Elizabeth II of England made him an honorary Knight of the Bath in 1993.

But with his widespread national popularity, it was inevitable that both the Democratic and Republican parties would be interested in him. His situation was similar to two previous U.S. generals—Ulysses S. Grant following the Civil War and Dwight D. Eisenhower after World War II—who rode their immense popularity to two-term presidencies. Would Powell follow in their footsteps? Many people believed that regardless of which party he chose, he would be elected.

But after a period of intense national interest, he announced his decision in December 1995: he would not run.

He continued to maintain a high profile in national affairs. In 1997, he founded America's Promise, an ambitious program to build the character and competence of this nation's young people.

And following George W. Bush's election to the presidency in 2000, he achieved yet another honor: he became the first African-American ever named as Secretary of State.

Within a year, he was confronted with a severe test of his political and diplomatic skills when hijackers crashed two airliners into the World Trade Center and killed more than 3,000 people. He had to rally worldwide support for the United States' war on terrorism. And on the home front, both he and the president had to make it clear that combating terrorism would not be easy.

After devoting nearly all his life to the United States, Colin Powell has earned the trust, respect and love of the American people.

"I have had a great life," he wrote at the beginning of *My American Journey.*

His fellow citizens would agree. They feel confident that whatever Colin Powell has in store for his future, he will achieve it with dedication, wisdom, leadership and honor.

Colin Powell has earned the trust, respect and love of the American people.

Chronology

Index